The Raven's Wing

Iain R. Thomson

Illustrations and paintings by the author

Inverness 2007

By the same author:

Isolation Shepherd.

The Long Horizon.

The Endless Tide.

Acknowledgements:

To Doug and Paul Haigh of BEGETUBE, Inverness, (underfloor heating specialists) for their generosity in providing desk and computer space in warmth and comfort. Special appreciation to John Slorach for his artistic eye, skill in layout, encouragement and good company. Sincere thanks for your help, cups of coffee and the odd dram after hours. Lastly, but by no means least, much appreciation to Annag MacLean, Gearadhmor, Isle of Barra, for giving me the courage to go ahead and publish.

Congratulations to printers, BigSky, environmental design and print, of Findhorn, Morayshire, on their presentation by Scottish Cabinet Secretary for the Environment and Rural Affairs, Richard Lochead, with the ISO14001 environmental management system standard, achieved after developing their environmental management procedures and their investment in eco-sensitive equipment and technology. This publication reflects the quality and attention to detail of their output, for which I heartily thank directors Lex and Karuna Le Feuvre and the team at BigSky.

ISBN 978-0-9536695-1-6

Published in 2007 by

Strathglass Books,
Cannich,
IV4 7NE
Tel. 01463 831293

Distributed by Strathglass Books.

Printed and bound by BigSky Environmental Design and Print
Findhorn, Moray, Scotland
www.bigskyprint.com

Contents

Contents

To
Jane, Molly and Sabine.

Raw the land without a tree,
Contours, slender, long,
Wave ground headland,
Hill and scree,
Pulse of strange affinity.

Storm split rock, blast of spray,
Wind that burrows in the face,
Empty space,
Un-trodden way,
Mindset of a northern race.

Midnight loom, solstice June,
Dimpled lochans, wailing call,
Treeless moors,
Land of the loon,
Arching sky, Valhalla's Hall.

Wind of northland,
Fjord ice flow,
Slanted wing,
White topped sea,
Is horizons sail.

Passion compelling,
Lodestones draw,
Magnets degree,
A predestined fantasy?

No place of birth,
Cradled culture,
Wealth or worth,
Deep the hold of DNA.

Untwine the double helix,
Decode it's formulae,
It will call you home,
Explain affinity.

Taken from, *Isolation Shepherd,* published 1983.

1   *Isolation Shepherd.*

The hill's wide sympathy of silence
Sweeps down by a far lost way,
Music of isolation and peace
Carries time to horizon's rim,
Where the wistful plovers call
Plaintive clear on a distant day,
Reaching harmony's only source
In the spirit of a single mind.

But gone is the ear that hears it,
Lost the breath of care,
Scattered the race to dreaming,
Fond eye to corrie and ben,
Heavy the loss that is Highland,
For the hills of striding men.
Shelter the glens that are weeping,
In the care of a single hand.

The curlew speaks of a melancholy that haunts the solitude,
From moorland space, in flowing note,
The diver tells of lochans, treeless and remote,
But the melody of the ouzel, amongst his echoed crag,
Sings the rich of yellow light,
Which brings the green of sheilings,
To the opal pools of morning.

The whisping trace of midnights chill,
By breath of kindled sun,
Is stealth of hand on corrie rim,
And in the hush of dawn,
A waterfall is born.

Mists are lifting, high tops clear,
Hinds are grazing deer grass dew,
Sunlight flames a heather ridge,
Yet dank below each moss hung bank,
Is still a world of silken bridge.

Stick and glass, the customed boulder leans his back,
A shepherd spies fox cairn and scree,
A ewe who could jink the day bleats from shelter stone,
Calls her lamb to an udder warm,
In the cliff face eyrie an eagle chick is still to feed.

Jaunty tails, a sniff, a growl, cocking leg and keen bright eye,
Collies meet, old black and tan, he 'woofs' and drives,
Broad white neck, the Border style, she controls by eye.
Grey muzzle wise and prancing youth,
An eager team, no grudging now the sore pad miles of yesterday.

Fine the day, sun on face, stiff the climb ahead,
Clean the air that powers the step,
A step that's fleet and swak,
No diesel fume or traffic roar,
Health, the lifestyle's pay.

The easy stride of plus-four tweed,
Takes man with tup horn crook,
To ridge which commands a view
Of corrie specked white with grazing ewe
And peak on peak, the workbench of a shepherd's day.

Dogs at heel, tight and quiet,
A ewe with twins spots his move, head snaps up,
A stamp of foot, a snort, she's off,
Bouncing lambs, the ewe, one backward glance,
Pell-mell along the face, a gathering underway.

Sheep below catch the sound,
Stare up, Which way escape?
"Way wide, good dog, keep wide, keep wide,"
She's round ahint them, five hundred feet below,
'Pinkies' pressed, a whistle shrill, " Sit dog, sit dog, sit."

Sheep turn, hurried tails, birling as they run,
" Steady now, good dog, walk up, walk up,"
She's a mile across the glen, collar white, hillside dot,
Voice and whistle bounce off corrie wall,
Nancy moves, checks their flight, two minds work as one.

Stubborn sheep, clever, sheep, deify a line of men,
Ewes and lambs make a dash, bolt between,
"Look out below," a speck of man, his bitch runs out,
Hunts them back on track. Others try the ridge,
Freedom break, turned by top man and his dog.

Antlers cross the skyline, click of hoof on stone,
A trickle flow leaves the snow, the drink is sweet and cold,
Moments pause and close beside, red crowned on winter's field,
A ptarmigan flutters unafraid, guards her crouching chick,
And way below in chambered cairn, a vixen and her cubs lie safe.

From midge free heights long trailing lines form an undulating flock,
Which rolls on down to lower ground, the river bend, a pony track,
Many miles, three thousand feet, and by the mid-day heat,
Heavy coated ewes will lie with watching eye, hope to dodge the drive,
And limping dogs, gut tight and sore will flop in peaty pools.

Bleating, bleating, high pitched lamb, low, the worried ewe,
Shouting man, barking dogs, a chorus fills the glen,
Lambs lost mums break and run, head for suckled slopes,
Tired dogs need goading shout, "Go back, damn you hold them now,"
A complaining flock winds down the track towards a captive fank.

Swing the gate, last sheep in, families join and settle,
Shepherds fill the kitchen, a bowl of venison soup,
Crack and banter, faces bronze, beaten by the sun,
Dogs in shade below the bench, rest nose on paws and sigh,
Tomorrow, if this weather holds, it's laughs and clack of shears.

How few now know the hill-man's life,
Birth and death at lambing round, the depth of caring for his sheep,
The hidden falls, a sun face glade, dogs asleep at side,
He spanged the tops, touched their stones, a glen below his feet,
The storm or shine of patterned cloud, scented birch beside the burn,
No landscape this of passing car, thermos flask or hiking boot.

No ticking clock his master, he knew the pace of wildlife's way,
The mid-night spring of north suns glow when snipe bleat never stilled,
A river bank where the tiny voles seemed bubbles as they swam,
The silence when the lochans froze and snowdrifts smoothed the hills,
And ewes came running at his call for meadows summer hay,
Sheep, dogs, hill and nature, companions in a shepherds day.

Sheep are shed and cock eared dogs lie gazing through the rails,
Neighbours gather, eye the sky, clouds are high, no sign of hurry,
They talk of tups that crossed the march, 'Aye your lambs are strong this year,'
Their humour has a subtle way, it isn't always what they say,
'Man, you've a nose to know the smell, you'll take tea, Jock, bacon roll?'
Jock turns slowly, foot on rail, four hundred faces gazing back,
'Roll? Aye plenty fleeces here to roll, what's the number of the dole?'

You've spat on the oil stone, honed your shears,
Rubbed them steady, back and fore, kept the angle true,
Tried each blade by feel of thumb, it tells you've got that razor edge,
Cast your eye across the pens, most ewes have open wool about the neck.
In darts the catcher, grabs the nearest to the gate, four feet brace,
Hand below he lifts her clear, by the end of day his back will know their weight,
He thumps the ewe upon her tail, you take a foreleg,
Part her lips, teeth tell her age, oval eyes look up in fear.

Lean her back against your legs, a grip of wool below her throat,
Balance is better than sheer brute force, she settles, takes a stoic view of fate,
In with the blades, down the chest, curse that belly wool,
It's tight and yellow, you wish she'd lost it in the heather,
Don't cut a teat, or slit a wedder's pizzel, he'll need it yet for peeing straight,
Now your clear, in the hind leg, go the long strokes, let it flow,
Bend that sheep, roll her round, sweep those shears, fill 'em full,
Old wool lies above the new, an inch of rise falls soft and creamy white.

Three sheep down, you're in the swing, catcher knows who's fast or slow,
Shirts come off, bodies brown, muscles heat to sunshine beat,
Panting ewes, bent backed men, sweat instead of suntan reek,
Five pounds lighter, wool away, a dot of buist, a jumping ewe,
Puzzled lambs bleat and sniff, mother never ever smelt like this,
But old Jock knows, he's spread each fleece, flicked in sides, rolled it tight,
Barefoot children pile them high, then snuggle down in smelly clothes,
Fifty still, a can of beer, 'dreeps'run down Jock's beaky nose.

Evening light on clipping marks, tidy, trim, ewes fresh and smart,
Open gate, lambs beside, white bleating trails climb a darkening hill,
Corrie heights fall silent at the press of night,
Sheep lie cudding, nothing but a flick of ear.

Hands that opened with a winter hack now lanolin soft as milk maids thigh,
Wash them at the back door tap, a bran sack towel hides the shite,
Neighbours, crofters, shepherds all, clack of tongues takes the place of shears,
A scrub top table, venison soup, a pan of tatties and inch thick beef,
Golden elixir in the Tilley light, tomorrow its down to Jock's if this weather holds.
Deer stalker bonnets, dogs and stick, 'tackit's clattering in the dark,
Stiff backs cured they spang it home,
'Man, that second dram was good.'

Ten thousand storms, rain, frost and snow had swept the strata bare,
To a curving ridge of shattered rock, an angled broken flow,
Alpine home to petals bright, no bigger than a farthing piece,
The pink and purple saxifrage hugged its cushion moss.
I strode the heights, dog at heel, autumn warmth on friendly stone,
No warning breath, rolling from the west, a white enveloped chill,
It cut my world, clung, shirt and hair, turned corrie depth to foe.

Bearing lost, I stood, wraiths stalked the ground below,
The dog raised cocket lugs, sniffed with trembled nose,
Suddenly, but yards ahead, wheeling birds in spectral flight,
Such union grace their soft alight, for tip to tip, long slender wings
Where raised in second's pose above each mottled back.
Gone the gloss of courting preen, their sheen of summer gold,
In place the grey of winter dress, to face each southward league.

Lonely throng, they shuffled feet in buffets vapoured swirl.
I felt their call, imprinted deep, since long migrations dawn,
Knew the grind of time below my feet, in nature's mighty claw.
No signal note, their stretching wings, arched tip to tip once more,
And silent as the mist had rose, they journeyed into night.

Elusive, far, a single note, wistful, fading, shy,
One plover's call, lone voice of space,
It gave a shepherd kingdom,
Beneath the open sky.

Diesel drench and lighted match,
Undo by single day,
Cared labours hand made years
Of deft cut stone
And shapely woods delight.

Searing heat, the timbers blaze,
Death by blood of fire,
Through sockets square,
Red eyes of pain,
Swirls the dancing flame.

Crackling loud, the rafter torch,
Licking hiss, the timbers crash,
Thrown wide to sky
Fond memoried walls,
To tears of bitter rain.

Acrid smoke cloaks the blue
In purple progress robes,
That proudly drape
Man's naked power,
To build and self destroy.

The hills of Strathmore.

Spit of stone to ember glow,
Trailing plume
To greet a night,
That wraps one bone in seeing thought
Of bare morn's laugh and scorn.

East sun shafts the windows hollow,
Black rimmed,
Staring, wide,
One final gaze,
To the hills of stalking days.

Charge of doom, an echoed roar
Explodes charred useless frame,
Whilst rumbled dust
Blinds watching eye,
To centuries' sad resign.

I often heard old Granny say,
'Sad the day we left the croft,'
'Yes boy,' she'd say, eyes far away,
'Gone the hand that guides the plough,
It's people parted from the land,
Two up, three down, a twelve by ten,
A window box and a frying pan,
No milk in the larder waiting skim,
No cow at the gate awaiting him,
Nor sheep, nor peat, or hens to lay,
Sad the day we left the croft.'

No grouse on the stooks, swifts in the loft,
Stacks to the yard or hay in the barn,
Before the first frosts coated snib,
Brought cattle calling down from the hill,
Hung collar and hames by the stable door,
Sent hooves to click the cobble floor.
Now it's gymkhana, polish and pony jumps,
Plough and cartwheels into ornaments,
A house with turrets to strangle the view,
Lawns and 'drinkies', late for the 'do',
'Sorry darling, stuck in a queue.'

Damn and flood now rule Strathmore's land,
The croft long gone, no caring hand
On meadows fertile, dung from the byre.
Pony cart and scythe cut hay,
Peats dug and spread, the winter's warmth,
Fish from the loch, a hind from the hill,
Survival in a bygone style,

West the strath, alluvial wide,
The bleat of snipe, a greenshank's call,
And deep inside a tussock nest,
Four spotted eggs in woven hide.
But water power put 'ads' on screens,
And we view wildlife by other means.

Hill and glen made Highland men,
Now laptop computers fill the roll,
Life styles change, land's second place,
Houses a religion, all view inside,
Dwarf, and intrude, elbow fields
To pony paddocks and rose bed lawns,
Smart 4 by 4's at the swimming pool.

Armchair ecologists, climbers, skiers,
Hills, plaything for some, a study for others,
Abuse and misuse ousts old respect,
Land and food no longer connect,
Global village feels increasingly tight,
Wise headman are sadly nowhere in sight,
Planet subjection, the order of day.

The hills of Strathmore are calling to me,
Have fun for today,
Climate change tomorrow,
Will have the last say.

Gone the hand that guides the plough,
Fresh crop has taken root,
Anarchy, the hollow grain
Will shed from rotting stook.

Taken from, 'The Long Horizon,' published 1999.

7   *Long Horizon, Lost.*

There's many's the mile,
O're many a stile,
But there's aye a hint-ward glance,
To the lang syne days,
And the old folks ways,
And the hills of the hearts romance.

No freedom roam to wood or hill,
Nor space to spread the mind,
No loiter in another world,
Which other beings find.

Yet summer's morn,
Down song thrush dawn,
On the road to work,
Twixt tree and dyke,
A shivered light lit hidden way,
For engines cough had still to foul,
The haunts of owl,
Before the edge of day.

Faint lingered shadows knelt,
Soft moss on tombstone dyke,
A hymn through vaulted beech,
To the leaf of autumn fall.
Grey pillared, doorway wide,
I stepped inside an echoed aisle,
Breathed its Holy incense,
Communion once held all.

Gentle on the sweet grass,
Below the tree lined hay,
A roe and bob-tailed twins so deft,
That every web was left.
And high amongst the branches,
Hide and seek and play,
Squirrels fluffed their cheeky tails,
Swung a schoolboy day,
And lifted heart, I laughed aloud,
And wished their simple way.

Often on the castle fields,
An ocean mist would drift,
And trunkless trees would float,
Upon a yellow sea.
And below the wondered pigeons coo,
Winding tracks tell-tailed the dew,
A meander here, a hurry there,
In a world that's seen by few.

And cows in silver coats,
Would rise and tend my call,
The ground was warm, a scent of milk,
Perhaps the wee folk knew,
For some once had seen,
The little men in green.

And for an inst. a blink of eye,
Ere sunrise filled the sky,
My mind grew wide,
I stepped inside,
Their tiny misty hide.

Cattle droving south fed factories nascent sprawl,
Coal and steel, the cotton bob, the clack of woollen loom,
Folks forsook the sickle, the flail, the damp of clay floor gloom,
Silicosis thraldom the alternative, a Company's 'double doom,'
Pulpits kept them suppliant, heard Empire's lordly boom.

Sheep driven north claimed croft and hill,
Hog and ewe to breed on 'mouly' ground,
No sweat of creel or hand sown corn,
Leaking ships sailed and lofty Nations grew.

Industrial 'toffs' arrived,
Self interest born of greed,
Lamenting land and kinship, people left,
Torrent, tide, a dream of better life.

Grandmother cried tears on crinkled cheek,
Burning thatch with child at skirt,
Her people went, on backs their bundled home.

Glencalvie wept.

A spring snow shelter, the gable lea of church,
Their last claim, a name on window pane,
My mother though MacGregor,
Young, I didn't care.

Sixty years without a thought,
Sunday drawn, I pushed the gate at Croick,
The gravestones called MacGregor, the window scroll the same.

The Minister preached, Absalum, my son, my son.
I knew at last, and cried on Granny's knee.

10   *The Piper Boy*

From Urchany crofts of Lovat land,
Men marched to the '45',
Ill spared toil of hill thin soil,
Some returned, some did not.

All waiting past, of quiet eve,
When shadows filled the land,
For sure at doors the folks would stand,
And pipes would sound across the greens.

Cnoc a' Gillie Phatean,
Hillock of the Piper Boy,
Lone boy of scattered race,
Yet in lament for Highland death,
His people still live on.

Faint mist upon the flats,
Lean winter stags to graze,
In changing light on indigo hills,
Hollows filled with evening's chill,
Were steeped in pinkest glow.

Steady on horizon clear,
Appeared the nights first star,
And stones of old Dun Mhor,
In memory stirred and mica bright,
The ancients built again.

Stone on stone, blood on blood,
Starlight and the spheres,
Matter, life, and spirit path,
All exists in endless cycle,
Creation and decay.

Time, mans own mythology,
Has no measure of the soul of being,
There is but change, death, rebirth,
Universe upon universe,
In immortal beauty.

I picked my way,
Old Nancy of the high top days,
Ever tight at heel,
Down through the Carnich,
The nightly lambing ewes,
Down to the warmth of kitchen light,
And children feeding orphan lambs,
In boxes by the fire.

11   *Sun Dance*

Four billion years has planet earth,
Danced to sunshine's tune,
Organic life should know the score,
The radiation theme.

For now the beat turns up the heat,
Life forms hasten, may miss a step or two,
Some may drown, starve, or flee,
The environmental refugee.

Can young 'h-sap' stand the pace,
Adaptive speed v. rate of change,
Dinosaurs could have told us so,
Adapt, old boy, or die.

Symbiosis? We've left that practice rather late,
Species stressed don't co-operate,
Twas a simple test of common sense,
Hom Sap's best mark, one out of ten.

The developed world has danced a jig,
Third world chokes upon the dust,
When societies mores become a riddle,
As Nero said, please pass the fiddle.

Inspectors, pen-pushers, in profusion,
Pass the day, stare at screens,
No degrees in common sense,
Working hands are scarce.

Politicians watch their backs and plot,
Planners plan, all press the profit slot,
Religions fight, Jews think their home,
Jehovahs nod, the end is nigh, it's the will of God.

Intelligence, ingenuity, now what's planned,
Space shots to the promised land?
Man's evolution stepping up a gear,
Robo brains, new genome,
Time to find a cooler home?

The race is on, adapt or die,
Or just sit back and fry,
Ingenuity versus wisdom,
Faith v. science sound,
Or trust old fashioned luck,
Turns up to see us through?

Perhaps the sun has help in store,
Beyond a tan for macho man.
Sunspots and dramatic flares,
Driven by vast magnetic fields,
Wax and wane through eleven years,
Yet each few hundred years are gone,
Before they surge again the maximum.

So when Sun's face is clear of spots,
Temps may cool and ice melt slow,
Might offset the flow of CO_2
Slow the beat of climate change?

Ten thousand past the pagans knew,
Sunshine spins the wheel,
Keeps larders full or bare,
So place your bets before it's dark,
And bow before the Sun once more.

Computer's down, conditioning's off,
Bloke beside you's got B.O.
Open plan, can't phone Pam,
Caught feet on desk the other day,
Half hour lunch, river bank,
Blink of sun to thank,
It's the hub of high finance.

Tube is crambed, doors don't flex,
Do you mind, O.K. I'll get the next,
Here it comes, pushing fumes,
Know the price of rented rooms?
She feels nice, rock and sway,
Read the Mirror on the way,
Look up, sneak a glance,
It's the hub of high Finance.

Jolly crowds, noise and chatter,
Even if one gets a trifle fatter,
On the bike, down the gym,
Expensive business keeping thin,
Nod, don't know the chap next door,
But a lively style, get the feel,
Tate modern, London wheel,
Pavarottie's at the Albert Hall,
It's the hub of high finance.

Sandy and I work at the lowly fence,
You may say, they must be dense,
Could be so, start of day, climb a hill,
No hurry, horizon clear, air has chill,
Shoulder carry, our tools of trade,
Punch and mell, hammer and the humble spade,
Wire and posts, we carried yesterday,
Dig a hole, pit a strainer, that's the start,
You may not think it,
Fencing's something of an art.

Line of fence, past that knoll, sight by eye,
Study ground, get the lie,
Hang the shirt, sun is blazing,
Now a little exercise,
Sandy welds the punch, heavy iron point,
Holes, nine feet apart, sweat on brow,
Not the bar he's at just now.

I swing the mell, fourteen pound,
Wooden shaft, round and round,
Hit the post, strike it flat,
Three inch down with every smack,
Muscles heat, trim and swak,
Man, man, makes you feel alive.

Fifty posts are solid, firm,
Sit a stone, oatcake, cheese,
Lie back, silence, enjoy the breeze,
The lager's cooling in the burn,
All day we've worked by Atlantic's space,
It's steady beat, made our pace,
And a pint at night,
In our favourite place.

Simple job? Wrong, there's much to learn,
Common sense, plus strength and knack,
Something finished, just a fence?
No hub of high finance,
Nor market crash,
Or game of chance.
Health is wealth,
What matters else?

Spray on tan, bikini's, sandals,
Fill those bags that pull by handles,
Try some ultra violet decadence,
Only farts say the planet's done,
Oh lay, let's rip the stratosphere,
Icarus, I think you need a beer.

Tarmac hits you, wow what heat, mobile phone,
Hello mum, it's pissing rain at home,
Dump the kit, lovely room, now the pool,
Lily white, newly here, you feel a fool,
Ten flights up, a balcony view of sea,
Join the tanning industry.

Marathon breakfast, saves on lunch,
Sunbed scramble, head for beach,
Towels and 'tranny', parasol palm,
Whites desperately getting brown,
Blacks wishing they were white,
Amazing sights, even frights,
The naked form in broad daylight.

Chips and fags, food and sun,
Pinta bellies belch and scratch,
Navel holes two inch deep,
Tattooed men, ten months gone,
Rampant bucks out for, er, 'a good time',
Muscle bound testosterone.

Oh, what 'boobs' come out to play,
Pert little ones, firm and proud,
Lift stiff nipples to the sun,
Massive pairs floating in the swell,
Tired ones, fed ten kids, played their part,
Other shapes, a credit to the surgeon's art.

No longer does that naughty crab,
Pinch the ladies big red bum,
It's half inch thong and two brown cheeks,
Jeans pulled tight at pubic height,
Glimpse of ankle, don't be silly, all's in reach,
Sex adventure, let's try the beach.

Plane towed 'ad' tells tonight's delight,
Foam party's on, lights are winking,
Spirits rise, beer is sinking,
Mowtown squeezes through the crowd,
Air is sweet, ah, the breath of blessed weed.

OK, the wealthy have their fun,
They've given the place a fair old run,
Why not just the ordinary chum,
Needs a break from tedium.

Here comes a luscious blonde,
Winding legs, and very fond,
She chucks her fag end in the tide,
Playtime planet, what a ride.

A barman's life is seldom dull,
As his clients get steadily stotting full,
Some are maudlin, sob and cry,
Others fractious, punches fly,
Girls are best, they scratch and bite,
Makes for a much more entertaining fight.

There's furtive guys who like confiding,
" See last night I gied the wife a hiding,"
Watch those sneaky eyes, he's passing dope,
Behind his hand, there's plenty scope,
Whilst in the corner being sick,
Can't take his drink, what a prick.

The music lifts a thumping beat,
Clapping hands, stamping feet,
Tables go, one chap is mooning,
Laughs and shrieks, women swooning,
The door swings wide, lets out the din,
In walks the 'Sally', rattles tin.

Keep pulling pints, wipe the bar,
The lap dancer hasn't arrived so far,
Perhaps she's detained by the boys in blue,
Wearing her dress for seeing through,
A merry night in spite of that,
No one's letting pints go flat.

Half-past one, "Last orders please,"
What the hell, who needs degrees?
Science, medicine, religious piety,
You've got one in psychiatry.

Mother really is so very tired,
Rumour has it, Father's fired,
Eight in one is rather many,
Especially when they spend a penny,
At least they can't jump on our bed,
Or Mum and Dad would soon un-wed.

But happy days are now in sight,
Tails are up and eyes are bright,
A pool or two, I mustn't fret,
We've got them on the internet.

There was one we didn't sell, every litter has a runt,
And Two Spot couldn't make it to the front,
Eight greedy mouths and no spare teat,
Needed helping Jane to gain your feet.

Still, around the plates you were pretty slick,
Gave each one a final lick,
Now silky hair, no scruffy tufts,
A prize one day at Crufts?

Plenty hyphens, posh pedigree,
And bearing in mind your family tree,
Two Spot seemed of low degree,
So we graded up your name,
And called you, Molly.

Taken from, 'The Endless Tide', published 2005.

16   *The Edge of Time.*

The summit cairn, a shepherd's hill,
I turned the glass, the sea grew in it's lens,
A silver thread, the islands long,
Luminous on the water, islands of the west,
I heard their voice as the cry of beating geese,
Which fill the moon with yearning,
And pass each machair spring.

I sat beneath the vaulted clouds,
Curved serried ribs, a creature cavity.
Gold sank to vermillion,
Blood of death before rebirth,
Seeped through sunset bones.

An orange path crossed the sea,
Pale peach sank to hallowed mauve,
Hills to blackness, headlands lost.
The circle of the sun grew round,
An eye upon the earth.

Far as twilight at the edge of time,
The islands fell before it's gaze,
And darkness on the wings of geese,
Slipped away to dream.

Wild heaving shoulders, ocean's strength,
Drawn by moon path's way,
Reaching arms, a turquoise bay,
A pristine waiting land.

Surging waves, the seed of life,
It's soul, horizons heart,
In main proud crests of potent foam,
They fall upon the sand.

Oh lucky wave, oh lucky strand,
For through each pounding thrust,
Is born a child of beauty.

Summer Isles astern, Stac Polliaidh's peak ahead,
Headlands dark, hills soft blue, lazulite the sky,
Islands rose and fell on a running swell,
Cormorants flew to ledges bright with sea pink bloom,
And mottled seals on skerries black raised chubby hands to scratch.
I sailed on, no landing here, stunted birch and boulder grinding shore.

Last moment, an opening, tiller hard a starboard, into a hidden bay,
A sheltered bay, no rolling surf, secure from the Minch's heave,
Above the shingle a ruin tucked beneath the bank, gable sandstone red,
Empty sockets, rafters on the floor, its roof to northern gale,
Lost, abandoned, a private home, fresh water at the fall.

The anchor dug in clean white sand, a curlew fled to a watching stone,
I swam ashore, sunlight spears turned pebbles into gold, and open eyed,
I watched the scuttling crabs on puppet legs, a world within a world,
What connections lie beyond, who says we near the end of knowing?

Cleared sea bed boulders made the rough stone pier, below a bothy door,
No more heavy nets to haul, no more salmon cobbles beaching on the sand
To land their silver beauties, dark tails a-tapping on the scale wet boards,
No voice, nor other human trace, possession vacant, to a dripping man.

Nettles cleared, I settled in, tarpaulin tent, and fish box find,
Till floating orb from shoulder hill, set boat in glass upon the bay,
And last of evening's call, the sandpiper sang beside my home,
Lisping notes along the shore, and rabbits munched just yards away,

The marble sea, the hugging sea, it whispered at my door,
I slept, the scent of earth below my head,
Nature's sleep, alive or dead.

19   *The Phantom of Consciousness.*

A stretching shadow filled the bay,
A shape, portentously,
No breath, nor sound, my boat lay still,
No tendril mist to hide a far-off shore,
The lordly hill reached out,
Dimensions crept a-quiver,
Where lay the haven of its power?

Stealthy kneel, thick water dark,
Tentative, I dipped a hand,
The figure slid away.
Could I but follow, find that realm,
The phantom of his consciousness?

Space, cell of equations exponential,
Who's photons fall, incandescent from a velum dark,
I watched the stars live but for a second on the still black sea,
Mirror of their span on the scale of cosmic birth and death.

Electrons, planets, atoms, suns and spiral galaxies,
Matter, a fragile skeleton for their energy,
If universe circles universe, are born to crash and die,
What place has puny man?

Hunched figure, primal rock across the bay,
Could he reach that apogee,
The coalesce of all conceptions,
Which is the pulsing system,
We strive to understand.

Arc of insight,
Encompassed boat,
A blackness, elemental, absolute,
I reach into an abyss, greater, deeper,
More penetrating than this earth's paltry night.

A spiral, spinning, tighter,
Faster, tighter, fast,
Tighter, ever tighter,
Crunching mass to energy.

An energy, heavy, heavier,
A density beyond man's science laws,
A heat beyond the n'th degree.

Time, ground to an instant,
Tinier than a measure,
The limit of dimension,
The inst that sets it free?

Fission or fusion, the universal forge?
Matter, antimatter, attraction or replusion,
Expansion everlasting, contraction to oblivion?

Dualism eternal?

War of the oscillating universes?

Dark energy or gravity?

Victory or annihilation?

No.

In domains of quantum gravity,
Infinite density curves time to space,
Where speed of spin defies the crush of gravity,
And time and space burst free.

There exists the rotating orifice,
Throughout which all has passed,
Through which all will pass, infinitus,
In bundled twist of braided space,
Which are the base of energy.

Imbalance heats magma's singularity,
On the anvil of understanding,
Entwining knowledge is the energy,
Powerhouse of the heavens,
Of all the universes that have been,
And all that are to be,
Imagination's pulse drives the circle of infinity.

Darkness settled into stillness,
The pressure of a silence,
Beyond the pitch of hearing.

A paradox surrounded me,
The closeness of endless space,
A space of spinning electrons scream,
Slowed to a hush, before the birth of time.

Somewhere, far behind the inst of man's emerge,
Somewhere in the memory of the stones,
A lordly hill looked down,
And hunched dark form, it wore insights silver crown,

Time beat ceaseless on creations shore,
And, clear across the water, a redshank whistled,
Three notes, three lingered notes,
Harking back in sorrow to a place where hope existed,
In the beginning, by a bay,
On the edge of understanding.

Where Uist ends and flowered machair,
Bound its sugar sand with knotted root,
There the purple shells were strewn,
And red-legged gulls bent their chocolate heads
Amongst the drying wrack, and shimmered day,
Eriskay, homely, green and gabled, lay across the Sound.

A Sound so thin and bright, it put a hand shield to the eye.
Sand blown isles were turquoise set, dark the Barra hills,
Sea highway once, raven sail and Holy cross,
It washed translucent to my feet,
The fabled tales which linger deep in Highland blood.

Air of primal age,
Breath of sea, tang of tide,
Filled the lung and mind,
Crystal cut, the ends of earth,
Atlantis in its majesty.

Horizons dim modern worth,
Shed pretensions hold,
I looked steadfast, sea to sky,
And thoughts dissolved to dreams.

Children of a Uist croft in ragged hand me downs,
Played the rock pools warm and blue,
Where ochre tangle hid the scuttling crab,
And starfish made their octopus,
And driftwood boat trimmed with feather sail,
Had wagging collies snap at lost reflections hold.

And childhood shrieks joined the cry of terns,
Which tipped and dipped, with forked tails spread,
To fish a sprat filled bay.
How little told these happy sounds apart,
On a sun dance day of laughing breeze,
Whose ripples barely stirred the rim of a listening sea.

Hand-holding, unspeaking, shyly from the beach
They came, watching quiet, a stranger at their father's croft,
Four, no more, one curly red-haired girl,
Safe behind her father's leg, with green eyed gaze,
Sucked the hem of a tattered turquoise dress.

Sturdy feet, brown with sun, no shoes that summer's stay,
Hardship, poverty, a child deprived?
Those children of the tide had a wealth abounding,
Countless as the grains of sand
On the beaches of their childhood.

My seat beside the road a cracked, back-broken boat,
Its wind-peeled planks of faded blue, thwarts of fading white.
Timbers ground, by a mighty coitus of the land and sea,
Sprung nail and rib from curving gunnels pride.
Strange it lay so far from home, abandoned memory.

Each evening as I passed a summer into autumns stately pride,
Auburn hair, dress sad torn, turquoise as the sea,
A raised arm waved, a dimple doll,
A childhood's doll, sat propped against its stern.

Nothing, nobody, child nor gale, saw her waste away,
Nor took her home in fond lament to learn again to play,
Did she know a childhood lost?
The sun would set in hazel eyes, unblinking eyes,
Unfocused on the present, a stare which held the past.

My bay-ward late met waving hand,
Put moonlight in her hair,
A dewdrop crown on auburn dark,
How oft we spoke, the doll in a boat and I.

Her eyes so bright with memories light,
Saw turquoise day, knew children play,
Beside a dune set bay,
And spirits laughed to see them count,
Each treasured shell,
Of childhoods golden spell.

The air grew thin with shadow short,
Another moon was waxing,
She climbed that night, white ice and crater pock,
I stood, tent by, her light a silver day,
My friend alone she floated, orb upon the bay,
My boat lay still,
Captive in the circle of her will.

Distant across the water, a quivered primeval wail,
Many piteous voices rose in shivered chill,
A sound, beseeching, sad beyond pure human grief,
Shepherds stick, I walked the shore, tense the brittle night,
Round boulders clicked, staccato, sharp,
Dead bracken rustled at my knee.

Unearthly music close, a trembled cry in pain?
A hideous mortal plight?
My breath coiled slow, damp and white,
Tinged the stealth of autumn's night.

Beyond the land, silhouette on moon-green sea,
Swaying, limbless, slender heads
Raised vibrant throats, and sang
Before the Goddess of their plight.

The People of the Sea,
Besought night's deepest pore,
Unlocked the sea-bound graves,
Of those who perished by an ocean's call.

I listened, the voices died, died to softest keening,
Lost souls within the chrysalis of their sealskin tomb,
Offered a coronach to life's ensnaring moon.

The Norsemen farmed the land beside the sea,
Sloping west and kindly lie, the ocean isle of Canna,
There long-house sites remain, mossy humps
That saw the panoply of life and heard the wail of death,
And here on a peninsular small, open, raw, does their spirit lie.

Not tame Sandray's dunes favoured of the southron folk,
Where friendly puffin nest the rabbit holes,
But here, under pagan sky,
Where the north wind rides the crests of Minch,
And the cutting spindrift blows.

And here, it's told,
A King of Norway lies,
Beneath the gathered stones which shaped his lifetime boat.

No spray covered his resting,
As it would in times of gale,
My day, in gentleness, saw pimpernels in bloom,
And in a hollow amongst the boulders,

I slept.

For the sea unrolling at my feet,
Had cords that draw the harp to a soughing melody,
And over fields of fledglings safely reared,
The skylark sang.

And the air made eddies of warmth,
Curing the hay for the people,
Filling their barns with the fragrance of meadow grass,
And the tiny flowers that yield their scent to a drying sun.

On the evening's stillness were the voices of the girls,
Calling, calling,
And the cattle came from the slopes of wild fescue,
Slowly on their chosen path.
And brown arms bent,
And golden hair tumbled against a mossy flank,
And the milk tasted of hills untouched,
And laughing eyes, blue as the sea, turned their gaze.

Time lingered, lingered as the note that waits,
Poised on the fingers of some plaintive air
That guides the pain of beauty into trance.

Ocean birdlife wheeled,
Their cry above unfolding ripples sigh.
The canvas filled,
A Raven croaked, but once, above the making tide,
A dragon prow nodded to the swell,
To a sun, alone above the Uist hills.

Northward trailed the isles,
Their skyline pointed home,
Took living eyes to a land they saw in sleep,
Beyond a sea they sailed by day,
To a sea they hoped to cross,
In tomorrows trance of death.

24   The Swinging Cage.

Limbs old bent, once entwined, and earth below an ancient larch
          knew loves passions flow,
White, the morbid strands where tousled mass spread golden,
          on the moss of evening light,
Gums drawn back, teeth stump black, eyes dark shadow dim,
          that had nightly shone alone for him,
Eyes, once blue as a longing summer watched the empty bay,
          faded now, to the loss of sea washed grey.

Through the open door, a birth bed cry, soon another hungry maw,
          the corner kist their only belly store,
Nine had cried, suckled nipples full and red, her last, no bed,
          they laid it out upon the hill,
No suck, a twisted neck, too frail to feed, she kissed its brow,
          and listened, the frost cut off his cry.
Softly as the winding sheet that binds, stealthy as a shroud
          which covers deaths infallibility,
She touched bloods newborn strand of life, felt its pang
          and crept into the night.

Haoled thrice, the moons white cloak turned sea to ice,
          bound their haven to a torpid shore.
Snapping branches, low swept by winters weight, made clawing
          arms of patterned light,
And crone of crones, her stumbled path tore knot worn hands,
          cut each barefoot slip.
Memories shed their veil, she heard a cry, a distant year upon the hill,
          'This night's child must live, by my sacrifice.'

Against the trunk she sat, crossed fingers on an empty lap,
        lolling head to aching sleep,
Yet through the pain grew summers bloom, and he came striding,
        blue of eye, boat and shore,
Needle scent she knew once more, lips their lingered touch, till shy,
        young limbs entwined below the crescent moon,
And children ran as sunshine brought its petal spring to meadows high,
        and longboats put to sea.

Tangled branches piled a crag above her tree, and year on year,
        the raven reared its early brood,
Two gawking chicks pressed tight that night, their heads hung low,
        no flesh to fill their gut,
Till scent on cringing air, deaths presence took its cold fingered grip,
        and gliding wing, a single croak.

Strike of dawn, bones iron to the ground, icicles her shroud,
        they stared upon a smile,
Her sparkled hair, crystal white, two sockets gaping red, no eyes,
        the chicks had got their fill.
Babe at breast, a grandchild boy, above the pyre of leaping fire,
        a rising soul joined the black of spiral wing.

Rope and cage, the cliff was scaled, one chick must have a wisdom eye,
        must join our family.
By ember light a longboat man, bare foot grip on horsehair strength,
        swung beside the ledge,
A raucous caw, the raven's wing, pinions beat, curved bill stooped
        close to rip his flesh.
A nestling crouched, black satan eyes shone from twig lined bowl,
        he grabbed, a vicious bite sank home.
That night, a willow cage hung beside the crib, dark watching eyes
        and newborn child were swinging, side by side.

Blue eyed manhood, bearded blonde, shoulders wide, arms
        to power a steer-board oar,
Though hands had still to take their knarl, a face its hook to carve
        by oceans cutting spume,
His father told, 'Our plough has scraped the rock today, worn horses
        shoulders raw, no land is here to spare.'

Twenty seasons the larch had shed, needle orange at its foot, axes rang,
        the crones tree sang,
'No gale has felled my sway, a north wind sets the Viking free,
        my strength goes with your ship.'
Cut and trim, she floated slim, by winter peat and oil lamp fantasy,
        a dragon tongue was carved to lick the sea.

May's the month of siren call, ages past its inner song knaws the heart
        casts an eye to far landfall.
Mutton barrel, rye bread store, hogs of ale and gleaming sword,
        he loaded thirty able men aboard,
Wives and sweethearts, skirts to thigh, carried their menfolk down the shore,
        shoulder high, one kiss, goodbye.

Crack of rope, the sail unfurled, wing tip wide the raven soared to terrify,
        sought carrion from a foe.
Slanted tight she flew, south by west her dipping bow, a rearing stern
        buried homelands snow clad sky.
Proud larch tossed the dragon prow, and high aloft in thumming stay
        Swung childhoods chick, wisdoms raven now.

Last evening light, the nor-east gale quenched a flaming sun,
        dashed crimson crests in steerman's face,
Feet braced bare, a pitching helm, 'The Raven's Wing' skimmed the sea,
        man and boat, bold mastery.

Moon torrent night is a sea nymph's tress, it's spray beguiling flesh,
        a sailors dream, yet haunt of treachery.
Spindrift coiled in shrieking moan, the gale to devils glee, the cage
        swung violently, a sudden caw, he knew the cry.

Swing the helm, full broadside wallow, sail crashed over, dipping deep,
        a pitiless wave trough hollow,
Crack, crack, split the mast, lee rail down, sail lay bellied on the sea,
        dragging stays, cage awash.
'Hack the mast, save the sail, to oar, to oar, head the swell,
        row boys row.'

Rope to waist, over side, diving deep, in deaths green chocking cave
        he caught the cage, held aloft the bird,
Amidst a tower of sea, an emerald plume, a burst of spray, a hidden rock,
        the tip of Orkney.

Angled hard against the crests, bending oar, young arm power,
        a dragon reared and fought the sea,
Flashing waves astern, a headland drenched in spray. Driven back,
        'Pull my boys, for mighty Odin's sake.'

Shoulders wide, one broken oar, a splintered wreck ashore,
        tormented gale, boom of cliff,
Backwash surge, he threw the helm, born seaman's touch put stern to sea,
        and down the western shores of Orkney.

Cape Wrath abeam, the Norseman's turning point, wide Minch ahead,
        an island chain, plunder, loot and gain.
Behind the Cape, Sandvarten bay, in they slid, beached her safe,
        beside four stravaging galleys lay.

Night time fire weaved spark and star, ale red face told their raven's call,
        wisdom for great Odin's shoulder in Valhalla's Hall.
Drinking horns, five would sail, the bird to be their guide, sword or strife,
        it's eye would find their home.

Roaring, roving, north winds terror, down the Western Isles, slashing axe,
        blood stained sand, the raven silent in it's cage.
Last headland, soft mist drapped an island hill, to lift by mornings glow,
        'Hecla, Hill of Shroud,' the lusty steersman cried.

Caw, cawing from a swinging cage, 'Loose its door,' the raven flew,
        a circle twice, it vanished in the sun cast shroud.

Village smoke, a turquoise bay, sand slope beach,
        Green fields to open sky,
An island home, a Viking home,
        By the old crones eye.

25   *The Raven's Wing.*

May's the month thin light grows strong,
Brings drumming showers brisk with sun,
Fills the air with scent of fresh tilled land,
Sends barelegged children to herd the byre thin cows,
Untied to kicking heel, beyond a dry-stone dyke,
And rolling pony's shed their winter coats on the heather slopes.

Vigour and elation lift the working day,
Men, a foot to cas chrom toil,
Women, kelp to wicker creel,
Stiff backs unbend, gaze to sea,
Isles stand dark, clear edged against the sky,
Summer's blue is yet to be.

May's the month for cutting peat,
On hill and heather bank,
Black trench below,
The smell of growths decay.
Father and son dig and spread,
An open hearth has greed.

North-east wind, keen to cheek,
Eye of youth is sharp,
A shout to father,
'The headland has five sail,
Slanted hard and drawing full'.
The father starts,
'The raven soars,
Deaths on wing,
Run boy, run boy, run'.

Down to the village by a curving bay,
Stumbled, panting, white,
'The heathens are on us,
Haste for your life, make onto the Dun.'
Women snatch up child, each man
The tools of humble land.

The Holy man blessed them,
'God speed you, save you,
I alone will stay'.
Galleys driven hard,
Rode the crunching sand.

Horned helmets, biting axe,
Leapt the dragon bow,
Waist deep, blonde hair flying,
Berserk the lust of killing,
Aflame in clear blue eye.

Broad arm, muscle, bare,
Gleaming blade,
A giant square,
Raised an axe to strike.

Island shrine, the Holy man
Knelt in Mary's prayer,
Nordic blue met Celtic brown,
Lock of passions eye,
'I forgive you now, my son'.

Thin skinny hands
Held Cross aloft.
One crash of axe,
A head split wide,
A Cross on sand,
Slippery, red and still.

The man who lived by north winds bite,
Stared long beyond the sea,
Would this clefted head step before him
On the pathway of his life?
Turquoise bay, one tide had turned,
In the immenseness of the day,
Would it flow again?

A sheer cliff track, creamed surf below,
Long climbing line out to the Dun,
Its neck of land their hope, would be a final stand.
Wide eyed children hugged crouching knee,
Their cave, Atlantic's boom.

The Sea Lords came,
The Isles men fought,
The tools of croft a feeble arm,
The neck of land meant life.

Sweep of sword, a blood slip path,
Crash of axe, a splintered bone,
Alive or dead, five hundred feet,
A falling scream to crunch of flesh,
In the slochd of tide black rock.

Evening's chill, by steadfast star,
A weeping trail took women to their bay,
The Holy man, a cloven head,
A trickle red, the drip of ashen death.

In anguished kneel, an old woman sucked its last,
'All the sand that ever blew upon this land,
Should not drink one drop of blood,
Born in Saviour Christ'.
Her simple act, a bridge,
The mists of Celtic creed,
The Cross of Calvary.

Fires aglow, the starlight dim,
Leather hogsheads slung ashore,
Drinking horn gave song,
Ale to wash the blood,
The women comely, feared for life,
The men of the North had need.

That night the women lay, below The Raven's Wing,
And hills black set on sleeping sea
Watched a healing moon sail upon their bay,
And knew the dapple light of morning sun
Would light by day, the path that all must tread.

Midst the sob of broken heart,
They spoke the words of a Holy man,
And silent men heard the women pray.

Four longboats took the morning flood,
One man turned, walked slow the empty shore,
Where a day before he ran.
Beside an open grave he stood,
They buried a clefted head.

Out by Hecla's cliff, Hilltop of the Shroud, the raven built,
Another brood was born,
And on north winds strength,
Sailed the eye of sacrifice.

The larch that knew love's pain and death,
Lay beached, till strand of life, his children sang,
And from it's steer-board oar, he made a cross,
And called the island, Mingulay.

Island found, Atlantic home, worn cliffs remoteness bound,
Spray and seabird cry, yet tucked where headlands ride the tide,
And plovers nest the sand, a beach which drew the dragon prow,
To the pace of wooden plough, harvest sun and crescent shoal,
And nets, jewel pendant full,
By morning's planet light,

Sunrise on a sea-ring sky, west by sail, lost to watching eye,
Fieldwork, bend, the aching creel, care, a women's day,
Bird cliff harvest, mackerel sea, peat to winter's hearth,
But danger, pain, childbed suckle, sea, oh sea,
Bring him safely home to me.

Then laughter played long climbing days,
Childhood swam the turquoise bays,
And honey filled the wild bee's hide,
Till flowered hill, full bird song mellow,
Rested turret cloud.

Then driving rain on huddled thatch, each winter dark,
Talked of thunder sea, and knee sat story fed young hearts,
To yearn the spring, a boat to set them free,
Free to the crash of a longboat bow,
The surge of a following sea.

Creative minds drove fancy's flight,
To space beyond the stars,
As lichen stones without a sun,
Crept into northern night.

When flake filled gale caked leaning birch,
And, red and green, Aurora's torch lit the drifted snow,
Then frost bound steps crunched to neighbours tread,
And dancing blue the firelight flames spun tales
Of sagas daring, told by old, late each wide eyed night.

Till sunshine spring brought blackbird song to catkined river edge,
And redshanks called and whimbrel probed along the worm cast shore,
Then shoulders heaved, stout lines were rove,
And milk-blue melt from ice capped hills,
Put longboats back to sea.

To tapestry days of shape and colour,
When perspectives long in mid-nights loom,
Are latitudes play on light and hue,
Each image turned to fertile thought.

The hollow wave, a cave of green,
The curl of storm, a sailor's grave,
Wind twisted branch, the waving arm,
That plucked its knowledge from the stars.

Ideas alive, fresh as the gleam of new turned soil,
That arched to the sun by creaking plough,
Clear as the air that drove their sails,
Sharp as the taste of gale filled spray,
Wide as the minds that sailed imaginations sea.

Where ends imagination's vein,
Are we miners of its seam?
A massless photon, energy's fastest source,
Out paces speed of thought, but wait,
Are there paths by which the insights stream,
Or some great emotion, may exist?

May travel, nay, communicate, by wavelength tracks,
Within dimensions which outpace the speed of light?
Does human enquiry, those striven constructs,
In exponential role, inflate, expand,
Become a force within the bubble of this universe?
Do imaginations boundaries grow?

Or is organic consciousness a dead end tunnel,
An aberration without a point or mean,
Does the universe exist to pander to our thoughts?
What may still emerge, evolve beyond this brain,
Atomic functions grow, without a carbon base?

As stars are born to spin the Hole of Death,
Within accretion's maelstrom disc,
So atomic amalgams yet may blossom,
The fruits of quasi-particle which swirl the stellar tomb,
Amidst the strength of gravity's cruel implode.

So Big Bang, were you a mega firework,
Spawned by a gargantuan Pit of Black,
Which halted energy's wild expanse,
And gobbled spinning galaxies, to crush by gravity's power?

Crushed, till density is the God who feasts on death of time,
And through the eye of singularity,
Sees twisted braids of space reborn,
To grow the waves of matter, for each fresh universe?

Atoms then perhaps are not as real,
Float only in the mystery of possibilities without end,
In realms where potential and uncertainty alone exist,
With frames beyond the myth of man made science.
Should all things be possible on an endless path of uncertainty,
This statement cannot then be true, to feeble logic minds.

A paradox stalks the framework of our brain,
We struggle to break the bounds of synaps' trap,
Its snail like pace of sodium irons, the neuron's organic grasp,

Unleash electro-magnetic's bending force,
Accelerate ideas beyond the photon's cosmic hold.
Release the God that we conceive,
Place a trace of 'interference' on ether's vibrant shore,
Manipulate the ghost 'entanglement' on energy's vast turmoil,
We are but what the heavens made us, in the arc of curving space,
And every particle therein is our kith and kin.

Let gathered knowledge short circuit creeping time,
Carry thought beyond constraints of man born mind,
Imagination become an oscillating wavelength,
A dimension in tomorrows space.

Will insights flash defy the strength of gravity,
Survive beyond the crush of density?
Imagination, wild power of consciousness,
That wide eyed child of longboat tales,
Will rove the seas of uncertainty,
And sail beyond this Universe.

A dram with Neil,
The hour that stalks the night,
I walked the bends from Ledaig round the sleeping crofts,
A bearing on my boat.
No voice, no car, a village prowled by silence,
In the spell of Heval's peak.

Thin, a fingered moon probed across the bay,
To dwell upon a hill,
A seconds flight by speed of light
Miles, two hundred thousand, more,
It's birth, four billion years in space,
Ten million tides till consciousness bore quest.

Two thousand years, a winter's tale,
One speck in time that turned
A humble birth to statued hill.
The spin of chance, or more?

That night it's light, a tiny glow, shone icy, death like, still,
Madonna and Her Child yet may die, of mankind's marble chill.

Late the year of hoist and trim,
Lone mast amidst the local boats, beneath a castle wall,
Curves encased in stillness, to each it's favoured course,
Till their mistress called the tide.

Echoed shadows clung, the Rock of Peter found,
Our Lady, Star of Fisher Sea.
Moon bright arms sloped from twelve,
'Each gale, the big hand slows', I often heard them say,

Cold winds of change blow from lava plain,
No distance now her dappled face,
As the sun illuminates her landscape,
So her stealthy beam, counts the tick of faith.

Pendants into circles, oars the drip of time,
Sinuous waters dark, the back of autumn seal,
In memory's grasp, so Nellie told,
A cub came crying, lost to Ledaig shed,
The boy who killed, in little time,
Was taken by the tide.

Empty isles, a hollow bay,
I drifted on a silver thread that laced the edging cloud,
That spun the steeple hands which hear the mortals pray.
 Indigo hush, oar measured drip,
 Intense the ushered change.

Cheek-brushed air, the merest breath,
Did carnal moon flesh wait?
Child in Arms, Seal Woman night,
Deep the myths that draw man to his fate.

Alluring she lay that November day,
Wrapped in the folds of the sea,
Gentle the fullness of her fields,
Smooth the flesh of curved white sand,
On the lap of a turquoise strand.

Temptress of a sailor bound
By wind-fresh scent, lip wet spray.
Lust will flow with ocean's sway.
As a woman's warmth drives an aching heart,
So the space of a lonely sea.

Steer by the main cried the wind's refrain,
Near, then far a seabird's cry,
A cry forlorn, a sorrow's choke,
As the hiss of drowning sea.

A mercy prayer of shipwreck storm,
The plea of last torment,
A soul amidst the wanton waste,
It whispered to a sailor,
Alone upon the sea.

Yet stronger still, above the seabirds mew,
The chaos in the wavetop light,
A piping wind in templed sky
Came calling, singing, clarion clear.

For that November day, I caught of countless memory,
A song upon the sea,
And pounding on the beach of Mingulay,
It beat the pulse of freedom.

A village bay in November grey,
Chain in hand, ride, plunge and sway,
I watched the greenbacks thump the sand,
Froth white fans on empty land.

The troughs are deep, swing her nose,
Anchor's free, a lee shore close,
Emerald seas, translucent light,
Wave crests turn in hollow curl.

A green surge under forefoot,
Rearing bow leaps sharp,
Now, I hurl the anchor,
Chain is racing out.

Staccato through the stem-head,
Turn on cleat, would the anchor hold?
Tight, slack, tight, slack, tight,
The 'Mingulay' boat could fight.

Black backed gulls came screaming,
Tilted wing and jeering,
I took the tension on the chain,
The anchor gave,
" God, it hasn't held."

I faced the sea,
A heavy wave,
Slow to break,
Up rose the 'Mingulay'.

Her stern struck first,
A shudder raked the boat,
Bow reared skyward,
I poised to leap,
Frightened she would flip.

She broke the peak, foam to waist,
A broadside swing, a violent roll,
It flung a sailor,
Beneath the curling sea.

Terrified, a trap below the boat,
I clawed from lunging hull,
Fell with gritty choke,
Soft moving sand dragged me out,
A mass of sucking foam.

I caught the chain, desperate cling,
Next swell would bury me,
If under an upturned hull,
Drowned for sure I'd be.

It came, white roar of measured strength,
A deliberate, open maw,
Swung the 'Mingulay's' bow ashore,
Washed me below her lee.

Green light above an open eye,
Green, the colour of drowning.

Coughing water, spitting sand,
I scrambled clear,
Ashore, alive, alone.

None to know, no message means,
Alone upon a beach, no other soul alive,
And pounding in the surf, my boat, 'Mingulay'.

Black rocks beside, the boat, moon-white on crunching sand,
I saw a phantom wreck, sail, gale torn, bodies flotsam on the swell,
Green arms a-waving, dragged beyond the horizon of despair,
Who shall divide the spirit of incarnation from the soul ascending,
Green the luminescence of the sea that night,
What voyage awaits us there?

I sat the stones where upturned boats once safe from winter storm,
No oil light chink of village door, dark gables fought the dunes,
Each gale, a spade of sand to cover hearths whose peat fire curl
Knew days of Celtic lore, the longboat sail, the words of Holy man.

Broken crosses made their shadowed angle on a burying mound.
Did walking dead of Viking time, arise to watch a moon
That oft it's magnet course upon the sea,
Had set their vision world a-moaning in the galaxy,
As the wind about me, in the marram grass?

Close the mantle of the island, spirit days of old,
Elated, as the lost return, I laughed aloud,
No outside world, no more alone, happy, home and free.
I watched the surf, its steady beat stirred innate memory,
Close as the living moon,
Reached across the sea.

Petrels tip-toed on the sea, dainty, dark, Atlantic chicks,
Flitting through the hollows, to nest at night, on the Geirum isle,
Ragged trails of terns dipped the Sound where the current streaked,
Along the cliff I fenced, their cries and sun for company, mine to know,
A longboat lay, chaffed hair plaited ropes, in the narrow sloch below.

Skipisdale, her landing, 'Valley of the Ship', the islands Viking hold,
Men stowed sail, bound a black wing tight, their longboat chaffed away,
And all the day I heard their voice in the swirling tides of Skipisdale,
A twilight name, I spoke it, saw the sheilings turn to smoke,
Saw the evenings wave tops bleed crimson by their sword.

Long combers in Atlantic's throat became an artery at my feet,
For Geirum isle, the hermit isle, had known a beating heart.
Who would scale it's cliff, turn moss chalked stone to Holy shrine,
What devotion would drag a man to isolations hold,
Who's wisdom thirst to desolations solitary cold?

Chapel of a single cell, did you bleed by Viking steel,
Or end as sun trailed time, helpless in its flow,
Or did your stone entombment survive, an inner cell?

I turned and saw the blue eyed children, a hundred years gone by,
By sea to school on Mingulay, words taught in the sand,
Back to crofting thatch, sail, or shoulders bent to row,
Arms and oars, along Atlantic's edge.
Tanned homes on Berneray.

Children, gunnel-faced, an open boat, across a open Sound,
Young minds on a journey,
Comprehensions sunrise,
Or sunset's blind embrace?

Burnished grew the heather, lit stones of sighting mark,
A puny tide crept below the planet's arc,
A symbol to the Holy man,
To cast this earthy shell?

Would his swirl of childlike faith,
Turn to seamless flow,
Or will it bow
Before the death of simple beauty?

Wave tops beat on Berneray,
Skipsdale lay dark,
Lighthouse beam swept the shrine on Geirum isle,
Fencing strainer on my back, I stepped home across the hill,

Old schoolhouse window of the days of childhood sail,
Shone bright with 'Tilley' light,
Archie had a supper on the stove.

Mingulay of the sea lay quiet,
And her voice, gentle on the shore,
Spoke the message of a Holy man.

Men who fed their families by the whim of the sea,
Who read its mood and knew its treachery,
Sailed south, a day of May, past the verdant Mingulay,
To cast their long line, eight hundred hooks,
Sou-east of Barra Head.

A gentle day, fresh and sprite, not heavy on the sea,
No man had stayed, home their holy isle of Pabbay,
Sail and oar alone, twelve miles out, the islands only boat.
One went unwillingly, a Barra man, by predestines hand,
For on him were disasters pang.

Hand over hand, rhythmic oars against a moody swell,
Line coiled aboard, cod and ling were the take.
Cool the air which pawed a ripple on each sullen wave,
Morning isles of starkest hue, became a bank of faded blue,
Pabbay slowly lost to view.

Fish guts cast astern, wheeling gulls fought screaming,
A wave top lapped aboard a laden boat, sneering, jeering,
Steel grey below the feathered sky, Atlantic's lip was curling,
'Cut the line, make sail, make sail'.

Lug canvas set put gunnel down, 'Reef her boys, reef her tight'.
Helmsman crouched, 'We'll run for home, hang out boys, hang out'.
They kept the lee of Barra Head, braced the channel twixt Mingulay,
Black, now roaring, came the fury, monster loosed that hid awaiting,
Satanic in the caverns of sea's cleft.

Sail brown billow, stitched by waiting hand, bravely drew them on,
Evil twisting, maniacal screeching, off the cliff top swooping,
Baring down, spume whipped to sky, hollow cheek and filling eye,
'Let her fly boys, let her fly', too late, the mast stay parted,
Canvas dredged the sea,
Gutted cod were floating,
The devil had his way.

Wound shawls covered mouths that gasped against the gale,
Howling foam filled wrath, it flecked heather at the feet of families
That apprehension's wake drove hilltop night to watch the sea.
Darkness brought no sail, daylight without a boat, the agony of despair,
The Pabbay men, breadwinners all,
Washed to Ireland's Saint Columba shore.

A Holy isle, far days before the Viking men drew keel upon its sand,
The sign of Celt and Cross of Christ were set in stone on Pabbays burial mound,
Though widows prayed in soft lament, no bodies staunched their tears,
An island without the manly power to haul boats above the tide,
Was left to wings that pass each hungry spring.

A girl, young and without guile, from Mingulay, long years before,
Sat gazing at the sea, alone a boat was hauling on its line,
Unfocused, mysterious as the trance of time,
She foretold the hunger of the Cuan a'Bhocain',
Hunger of the 'Sea of Ghosts'.

Faithful each year is said a Mass, the old beliefs, again of mystery,
Are murmured at the altar, for the souls of Pabbay men,
Our Lady, Star of the Sea, hopes blind statue,
Wishful as a night of gale,
Or mystic as the 'Gift of Sight'?

33   *Earth's Bounty.*

Trouser arses wear before the knees,
Drooping bum cheeks wobble,
Bellies advertise the hop field pleasure,
The click of tickets, kill the clack of shears,
Sheep are out, tourists in.

Islands that held a race made hard,
By sun bent backs to oar and hoe,
Are alive today in digital glory,
The plunder of a purpose,
To the laptop screen.

What the loss, what the gain?
No harshness when a winter eats the grain,
Lambs made lifeless by the sleet,
It's lunches packed, a themos brew,
MY, it's SUCH a 'LOVELY' view.

Cultural change is on the rampage,
The jaundiced eye of age won't allow,
That earth's bounty is of ample food,
To let kyacks paddle round the bay,
And 'trainers' trip where Viking leapt.

Empty dunes, no skylark now to hay tanned fields,
Just the passing tramp of feet,
Deep the soul where lost culture hides.

34   *The Dunes of Allasdale.*

Twin rotations spin, floating north the sun,
To rest one night it's Solstice light,
Twixt two simple gabled crosses,
Guardians of a Faith.

White by day, pure before the cobalt-blue,
Straight the roof that heard them pray,
The evening cross stood black,
Against a blinding eye.

Who will put a bridle Atlantic's might?
Royal by day to fragile duck-egg blue,
It fades as last north night,
Is blood upon the sea,

And there upon the shore,
Faith lies in it's foetal form,
Bones within the circled stones,
Shifting ever, as the dunes,
Of homely Allasdale.

Dawn till dusk, throats are slit, on the road to Nazareth,
Wait and watch till each turn approach, men and women, crying child,
Three thousand Muslim, a chained and beaten foe,
Crusader victor, raised a jubilant dripping sword,
The chronicler wrote, midst spurting blood, 'Rejoice, rejoice,
They died to the Glory of Our Creator great'.

From stygian grotto, oaken glade and caves of flickered light,
To soaring stone and altar pomp, the mark of doctrines hold,
Man's weakness in his fear of death has fed religion's grip,
Each sect secure within it's branded truth pays faith and homage,
To their special god, styled by the pundits of divine certainty.
Pyramids of power built by purveyors of spiritual inertia.

Omnipotence, incomprehension, human fashioned gods,
Infuse the unknown force of being with a bogus reality.
However staunch belief, acclaimed, worshiped or beloved,
Gods evolve, and history tells us all concocted Deities have their day.
Past records show, God today is doomed to be tomorrow's myth.
Norse Odin, gaining knowledge for an eye, foretold all gods will die.

Soil to sky, rocks to rivers, flowers and trees, all life's form,
So Celts did say, so Aborigine walked 'Song Line' into 'Dreamtime',
Human life existed, one integral element in a holistic world,
Now monotheism fuels the flames, set mankind apart,
Some believe they are the chosen few, God's anointed right,
And cluster bombs take children's legs whilst pious leaders pray.

Budding dictators form a queue, to force democracy,
By means which hasten its demise, secret torture, state control,
Pre-emptive war, the suicide bomb, terrorists for one, hero another,
The centuries pages tell, freedom dies by force of arms,
To rise again by slave revolt, the stage revolves, misery ever in the wings,
And always, the terrorists within who run the Ministry of Fear.

Religious 'truths' compete, some preach blind certainty,
Muslim martyr, Evangelist, Armageddon, Rapture for the few,
Eight hundred years, still the blood runs down the road to Nazareth,
Humanity cringes before the screen, then wipes its lily hands,
And leaves the carnal mess to a tiny caring band.

Virtual reality becomes our norm, outdoes what once seemed real,
What price now religion's patent truth,
Is good old God obsolete,
Cruel, outdated, crude,
Illusions contorted soap,
A theory no sounder than the dope?

Shuffle genes,
Play the code,
Restructure our intelligence,
Will that stop the bombs,
Who will intervene?

Certainty defies un-certainty,
What have we but hope,
A flawed and empty value,
Or the road to truth?

36   *The Retirement of a Westminster P.M.*

Column dodgers launched an illegal war,
Christian banners waved, shielding eyes
From waiting death and limbless maimed.
Brilliant strategy, spin a story, the 45 min. bad boy,
He'd shown the way, spread entrails across the floor,
Praise the Lord,
Our cause received a sound applause,
From the Holy selection board.

Two flags entwined had White House chanters on the lawn,
Saw forelock tuggers fawn, avoiding bullets, reaping glory,
Bagging contracts, arms and oil,
Brave the bunker 'guy' who invented, Shock and Awe.
Win hearts and minds, needs just a little force,
Praise the Lord,
And pass the ammunition,
Depleted uranium, if you please.

Baghdad paints the sky, gee guys, see 'em fry,
Spray walls with blood, there's families in the way,
Blast those murals telling civilisations dawn,
Killing today is such a refined art form.
Torture? Now there's a clever tool,
'Extraordinary rendition' here and there,
So praise the Lord,
We need the truth, useful thing,
Beat their balls make 'em sing.

War 'tis such wondrous ploy, lets politicians feel their power,
Tiresome people demonstrate, so turn the screws on democracy,
Votes old boy, my press will handle such a boring chore,
And don't forget, my memoirs are on the way,
Should salt a bob or two in the bank.
So 'rejoice, rejoice', as mentor Maggie said,
Praise the Lord, thanks giving at our shrine,
Sad the legless orphans pay,
I must turn my righteous head away.

Messiahs come, Messiahs go, are you one, it's hard to know?
Can one judge, did our soldiers die to support your vanity?
Ex- thousand dead, nightmare and pain, could it all be in vain?
For certain, hypocrisy is a handy trim, saves the snag of looking in.
Well, bye, bye, Tony, brilliant legacy, a knighthood's on the way,
" So good Lord, praise apart, you know I did what's right,
Pity things went a shade 'aglee',
If only they'd listened more to me."

" Going to make a hit with my guitar,
Caribbean home, I'd love to be a pop star,
Meantime, let me see,
Fresh fields and pastures new?
Waiting list? I'll jump the queue,
Save my soul? One can't live on hope,
I'll get absolution from the Pope."

Driftwood built it's counter,
Wreck and plank it's walls,
Fish nets hold the palm leaves which thatch a snuggled roof,
And each day the tide white sand is spread upon it's floor.

This shanty has no garden need,
The surf that brings Sahara's heat,
Is doorstep, brush and bell,
And Marley throbs the fire-fly night away.

And wits compose by candle light, scrawl upon the walls,
But eyes entwine and saucy smiles fall on turquoise scrolls,
Wild dreams are stirred, sly fingers stray,
And then the fun brings.

For who would put a measure on a tot of rum?
It fuels the evening's jig, elixir by the swig,
And once the crowds Nirvana bound,
Shy maidens cant be found.

Beware, oh bashful reader, avert capricious eye,
For now's the hour a carefree moon,
Leads maidens to it's path,
And pants and bras are hung.

And laughing nymphs with ivory bums,
Are luscious shapes which hand in hand,
Scamper down the starlit sand,
For who would clothe young Nature's ploy,
Not sailor lads like me.

They plunge and folic, laugh and squeal,
The music beats, lazy man, my how it seeps,
And nipple proud the dimpled sea,
Lets wicked little moon drops fall,
Upon each secret curl.

'Til wave tossed, dripping, out they come,
And smiling teeth with brown faced gleam,
Hands naughty 'Tee- shirts' cling,
To each enchanting form.

Ah me, this wanton beat my dear,
Fair lifts your dancing feet,
I fear your 'Tee-shirt' treat, my love,
Is just a trifle neat.

Who invented things that sway,
 Eyes that flash the night away?
What sailor lad would think to sleep?
For youth and beauty seldom keep,
A lock on Paradise Door,
And those who lift it's latch and peep,
May sail the endless deep.

A fitful wind idled in our sails all day, and heat,
Oh boy, the deck, t'would put a blister on your bum.
David Jones, our Virgin Islands weather watch, and not a name in jest,
Droned his plumy voice that morn, six hundred miles away,
'Well chaps, nothing untoward, my screen say's all's O.K.
What's the wide Atlantic like?'
'Hot and stuffy,' was Skipper Rob's reply.

Strange to say, by watch at four, the glass seemed firmly stuck,
It's needle not a move,
Yet sullen air had wavelets a'smacking at the hull,
It took an unusual chill.
Hard astern, nor-west horizon pressed heavy on our boat,
Rolls of cloud puffed high and wide,
A grossly weaving shape.

Soon red and orange searchlights probed the upper skies,
And flicking shafts behind a thin white band,
Advanced across the sea.
A sea so dark, the darkest navy blue,
Held on it's rim, a charcoal line, a line of solid black.
Fresh clouds made purple cushions, laced with silver edge,
For sure I thought, they had the old sun trapped.

'On the Road to Mandalay,' I turned to shipmate Anne,
' Was it dawn or evening that came up like thunder,
 Out across the bay'?
Six eyes gazed aft, no lightness in their stare,
This could be dodgy stuff,
The thin white band and line of black,
Turned to churning sea.

A rifle crack, sails snapped to life,
'Down the main,' a shout from Rob,
Anne at halyards, braced and flying hair,
'Jenny now,' he called,
I hauled, cut the canvas spread,
Astern, the forked barbs tore.

Great ponderous clouds, full belly black,
Split, the crack of splintered glass.
Flashes, one, two, three, again, again, again,
Each lit a mass of wave top, yellow, navy, green.
Illuminated seascape, a palette spilling paint,
Unlikely seadog's tale?
This time we saw it real.

Thirty thousand amps from heaven,
Rob raced down below,
Pulling fuses, switches off,
Hit our mast, one shot of this
Would electrify the lot,
Blow a hole clean through the hull.

Wind hit, sudden, hard, gusts to forty knots,
Our 'jenny' took the blast,
Once, twice, too much sail,
'Winch, winch,' bawled Rob,
'Don't let the headsail blow'.
At fifty heel, you bet we winched away.

Billows black at masthead height,
Darkness trapped us full,
Crazy, zapping zigzags,
Each seconds blinding flash,
Lit a spiralled sea.

'What distance that one?' thunder cut the voice,
Count the seconds, nil, another deadly fork,
Simultaneous, overhead,
A thousand welding arcs.
Plunging into sea.

Eardrums took the pressure,
Cordite filled the air,
We raced across a foaming pond,
We must be hit,
Next one could be it.

The gale forced us on it's path,
Rob fought the helm, arms out, ripple straight,
Hold on, watch,
Count each flash,
We'd counted naught, but luck.

At last the storm pulled south, last grumbled roll,
Dawn came, bleakish, grey,
Wind fell light, we sat a cockpit cup of tea.
Noise astern, Anne looked up, 'Oh s--t',
Out of haze, the frenzy of a herring shoal.

A waterspout behind the storm, a writhing coiling snake?
Instead, rain, torrential, warm, came thumping on the deck,
Bodies brown peeled below a shower, soap and Anne's shampoo,
Washed salt and night's concern.

Rob rewired our set, and sharp at ten, the 'Locker' spoke,
'Did by chance a storm pass through last night?'
'Sorry, didn't catch it on the screen, had a look,
How it arrived seems quite a fluke,
Your course today, now let me see'.

Atlantic sail, by computer track, we dismissed as boffins knack,
But 'Davie Jones,' though desk bound at his screen,
Now, that had a ring of re-al-ity.

Civilisation is a sand castle on a lineal cosmic beach,
Science says we're just a primate, with a clever reach,
A gift for ingenuity, a step on evolutions adder,
Two million years, Olduvai put us on this ladder,
But the God slots hold up hands in prayer,
It's only six thousand since naughty Eve was bare.

Which turn now the flock will take,
Who control our slender fate?
Preachers with an eye on their salvation,
Egg heads bent on new creation?
What hissing snake lies in the grass,
Awaiting the human foot to pass?

Two pacifist creeds come to blows,
Give us all a nuclear bloody nose?
Ego leaders of religious certainty,
High on hope, is it dope?
What solution to the planet's bug,
Pray to God to pull the plug?

How long before the womb is obsolete,
We fuse animate with the inanimate?
Genes, our latest fruit machine,
Stop the one with an IQ lean,
Replicating robo with quantum computing brain,
Have a cuddle, it could be sane.

Please God give us time, tricky one this climate change,
Sun shade discs in space, sulphur in the atmosphere,
Meanwhile our latest probe could mine water on our neighbour Mars,
And a particle accelerator build a mini black hole,
First step to a fresh universe.

Let's grab a little hedonism on the way,
Pity the old environment has to pay,
Planet play station has no reverse,
Clever stuff, or some God's curse?

To a sailor on Atlantic lat. a setting sun has much to tell,
Day by day, his massive orb lowered gently in the sea,
Sometimes his orange tip shone through horizon's rim,
Lit the jostling waves with a flash of vivid green.

It gave us settled weather, a breeze to drive us east,
A deck of warmth to lie and watch the ocean world,
Where beside our hull, on tiny slim pink sail,
The Portuguese Men o' War went a-voyaging,
Chartless on their cosmos, at the currents whim.

Without warning dolphins skipped along, and in mid-air twists,
I met a knowing eye, no fish un-seeing stare, but warm,
As though a bond has held us since aeonian time.

I lay, face up and bronze, clouds drew patterns on the sea,
Marked our course, lightest blue to dark marine,
Sometimes, without reason they chose a deep, deep green.

And only the swishing of our bow, a dipping, dipping, dipping,
And all the day the mast made a sundial on the deck,
Till angled rays lit our helm and faint on its smooth edge,
Shone the evening star.

The sea took on a purple sheen, and so our Venus shone,
A pencil line of brilliance joined us to her power,
And for a second, before the shutters of a tropic night,
We sailed with her alone.

By ancient tale, great Zeus, God of Gods,
Begat this lovely daughter, sprung her from the foam of sea,
Goddess of love, she kindled lusts in a setting sun,
And through the privacy of a union, in halls beneath the earth,
Was born the swelling fertile moon.

Myths, once our sacred lore, are milestones on a journey,
And facts today are the myths which point tomorrow's climb.

Mid-night watch, before the moon could peep across a treacle sea,
Fourteen lights glowed amongst the stars, flying tail to tail,
Planes on track, smart bombs, Middle-Eastern bound?
Blast apart a civilisation whose Babylonian days,
Gave us calculations which sent man's footstep into space,
Intelligences' route or a mindless cul-de-sac?

The Milky-Way was mast head strung, no blur,
Miriad pinpricks bright, of such intensity they stretched
The broad band of our galaxy across the darkest sea.

Will spiral arms uncoil and spring like,
Fling apart the matter of our being?
Will energy's black sink
Find power enough to rewind its centre core?

Could information be its concentrate about a hollow coil,
Be intelligence's flow, that sails the eye of singularity
To another universe, dimensions different, reality new born?

The sea made undulations slow and on its mirror curved,
I saw reflections of the heavens.
Theories grew beyond control, and thoughts unchained,
Wandered out-with this planet's hold.

The breeze toppled simple waves, made small white flurried foam,
Black shapes leapt amongst its brightness, first a distance,
Till cavorting round our hull came each a shooting golden glow.

The moon arose, an orange hoop of play,
The dolphins raced to greet her,
 Silhouettes upon her face,
And with them went my heart,
To join their humanity.

On visiting King's College, Cambridge, with William Dick.

King Henry the sixth of England, granted powers to Reginald Ely, Master Mason, to impress workers, on pain of imprisonment, for the building of King's College. A number fell to their deaths.

41   *The Final Stone.*

Now lads, it's climb or jail,
Hoist those stones, shoulder up, now raise,
The job you're on must not fail,
The God I serve is lapping up my praise.

No yellow head gear, safety belt,
Who placed the final vaulted stone,
Was prince of a humble world above,
Worshipped by the pompous souls below.

Oil put a rainbow on the puddle,
Showers past, or more to come?
Found a particle on the sand,
Glowing green, quite a find.

A plastic bottle rode the flood,
The oil slick drifted where the wader stood,
Once there were thousands,
Now there's one.

A redshank, by it's triple note,
I stepped in sludge, the bird took flight,
Tail feathers flash, a bonnie white,
So what, it's on the 'tele' tonight.

I was born in thirty-three, two billion on the stage,
Six billion now, and rising rage,
Lifestyle of the wealthy leaves a legacy,
The poor just remain in beggary.

Man or bird, all life forms take their chance,
The selfish gene has no romance,
Climb the heap, no single file,
One dirty, almighty pile.

In case there was a message of some import,
I opened the bottle on the beach,
No word, but a yellow curling fume,
And stench, it would clear the room.

Last redshank thinks, strange, there's still a tide,
That mollusc had a funny taste.
Stupid ignorance, or is it bliss,
No matter,
There's a show tonight, we mustn't miss.

Five billion years, red giant Sun will blast this comfy niche to smithereens,
But a seventh extinction looms, long before its swelling mass,
Boils our oceans dry.

Except for cunning virus, life-forms peak and die throughout this planets history,
Tomorrows crash is organised by a slick humanity,
And as the earth is weary of our race,
Fly me to safer place,
Mars a passing rest,
Find a cleaner nest,
Attempt to seed the universe.

The braids of space, dimensions splice,
Are threads of possibilities infinite,
And life, the throw of chaos dice.

All that has ever been, that may ever be,
The matter, time and space of this present universe,
 Is crushed to single eye, a spin beyond the speed of light,
A density, the sum of all reality,
In the grip of gravity.

Magnetic frictions glow, matter melts to energy,
Atoms heat to un-guessed degree,
A particle flux fills the cusp, a coiling hissing pit,
One inst, a nano-seconds flash, imbalance strikes,
Blinds the eye of singularity,
Its matrix bursts, electrons flee, a universe is born,
The ghostly holograph of all eternity.

One force survives, un-diminished through the eye,
By some strange ethereal affinity,
As an echo, universe to universe,
Is entangled photons flight.

Speed, nor distance, nor realm of space, separates their bond,
Each qubit of existence has its partner mate,
That defies the un-ending nihilistic twists of fate.

All being in whatever form, is but a wavelength drawn,
Consciousness, the path without a bound,
Imagination, its dance before the sun,
The mystery of entanglement,
Our circled bond in space.

No more the stink of tattie rot,
Starvation at the door,
Hollow eye and lice rid smoke,
Bare feet on earthen floor,
We've eaten of the peeling,
Walked the shell fish shore,
Hope is on the wing love,
Time to face the sea.

Child on hip, bundled back,
Tomorrow it's the New World,
Come my love with me,
We'll leave behind the Old world,
A tearful melody.

No more to stranger laird I'll lift my cap,
Beg a stack of peat,
We'll fell and clear, log and build,
Dig in freedom's soil,
Spade and axe, muscles bronze,
Carve our home by toil,
And when the harvest fills the granary,
We'll dance an Irish jig,

Perhaps, my love, by gloaming light,
There'll be a wee romance,
Hearts will bind, our bairns will thrive,
Sure luck will give us chance.

Sugar sacks and black men filled the teeming wharf,
Fog the Mersey wide,
Captain Mason took our passage fee,
We stowed below the decks.
Gruel and water butts, his brig the 'Annie Jane',
Beat into September sea,
Outward bound North Channels tides,
Put Irelands coasts hull down.

The first gale took us, a topmast split,
She wallowed round, ran for repairs and safety,
Liverpool grey, all money gone, we gazed at spires,
Pious wealth, against our poverty.

Make sail again, west the Hebrides. Mason was a driver,
A man who'd run her toe rail under.
The wind had 'tain a sou-west slant,
Seas a watching curl,
Clouds were spiked with thunder,
As slow there came a thrumming,
Drew the rigging taut,
Set her timbers drumming.

Below the creaking decks,
Crouching children listened,
Vomit filled the stagnant air.

With a scream the Atlantic gripped them,
Crash, the mizzen fell,
Crack, her canvas split,
Heaving topsides dipped the sea,
Lockers burst, water poured,
Emigrants lay in misery.

'Man the pumps', rang from the bridge,
Seas cascaded down the deck, bilges were awash.
Three days, in relays the emigrants pumped,
The 'Annie Jane' rolled, beam to breaking sea.

Last glimmer of September light, a masthead shout,
White the glow of bursting plumes,
Fang stark the cliffs of Barra head,
Lit by moon glints Devil horn,
The terror of lee-shore.

The gale howled gleefully,
Throw the helm, claw us south,
But yards were dipping sea.
Rolling, pitching, two helmsmen at the wheel,
She swept below the tower black cliffs,
Of desolate Mingulay.

Spume lashed rock, wind piped symphony,
Heads craned,
A mighty backwashed surged them clear.

Water swirled the cabin floors,
Children sobbed and retched,
Mothers said their rosary,
Men hung in the rigging,
Breath sucking, hands without a feel,
Was this the God who led them to a promised land?

Driven north, hope still glimmered,
An island channel east?
Through the mad cacophony,
Of sea enveloped sky.

Mid-night hour, she struck,
Toppled masts, timbers rent,
The first wave took those who clung,
The second drowned the praying souls below,
The 'Annie Jane', lay pounding, a splinted wreck in three,
On the sands of Vatersay.

Dawn came hodden grey, desolations gnawing wind,
Emerald curls their passion lost, each impending hollow,
Fell with sorrows boom.
Three hundred, more,
Another land of hope.

Spade and carry, hand dug dunes,
Gently, side by side, mother laid with child,
Last hug, beneath the sands of the lone Traigh Shair,
Their blessing mass,
The fretting wind in marram grass.

Can we construct an objective reality that's outwith our conscious form?
Pythagoras thought the universe a complex mathematic trick,
Galileo believed it a 'grand book' of arithmetic,
All maths and their equations an abstraction,
An immutable existence outside,
Constraints of space and time.

One hundred billion stars and their minions swirl around each homely galaxy,
Calculate the relationships, the spin of stars to tide washed grains of sand,
Construct equations which reach beyond evolutions cosmic crawl,
Tap systems at speeds where universal time slows down,
Where the particles which build all present states,
Exist in two places simultaneously.

Only then might we judge mathematics has become a function of the flow of time,
That needs the theory of a multiverse to make logic predictions tick,
Each it's own set of rules to account for variability,
Chart the elusive course of probability,
The cause of our uncertainty.

Maths, the elegant geometry of space, a deterministic tool, lacking freedoms supple flex,
For on the beaches of our consciousness wash countless grains of time,
That change with every tide, with every fresh born galaxy,
Whose mineral palette is the swirling photon brush,
That paints the beauty of the cosmos,
As loves simplicity.

In Viking times flowered meadows spread to Greenland's open shore,
Waving grasslands, the herring shoal, wild berry store.
Iceland's longboats sailed, farmsteads grew, churches built,
Not that Norsemen were of a praying ilk,
Adventure was their stock in trade,
Land grab followed daring raid.

The walrus hunters of these northern climes,
With sealskin boats, killed a helpless prey,
Clubbed the lumbering sea cow to extinction,
Sold ivory tusk to southern wealth,
In turn their death arrived by Raven sail,
Eric Red, not a boy to spare the blood,
Built stone houses where hide huts had stood,

A millennium past, and Greenland's sword won spoils,
Were covered by an ice caps slow advance,
The North-west passage froze Atlantic's door,
Left wilderness to polar bear, igloo and the seal oil lamp,
Few survived the ice sheets crackling merge,
A land of fog and drifting berg.

History is a repeating drama,
Fresh actors mount a revolving stage,
Calving glaciers swell the sea,
Passage opens, ice free soon,
Global warming, trading boon,

Below the sea where longboats fished the teeming shoal,
Where hunters took the Narwhal's spiralled treasure,
Nation's eye the Artic oil,
Another raid,
Another spoil.

Deer tracks crossed the watershed, sure hooves that angled steep,
Into far Lochaber, where a corrie space fed the eagle claw,
By calving hind and ptarmigan ridges bare,
Where torrents streak each hanging rim,
And hidden fall, loud, then soft,
Was the music of the hills.

Highlands of the savage scene, loch of Nether World,
Narrow waters of Loch Hourn, oft of wind torn sea,
Where days of gale lift spiral sheets to pouring cloud,
That rent upon the precipice,
And set it's jagged rock,
A bellowing, as the fabled bull,
Of old folk mystery.

Waters where the stalking peaks lie still, as gathered shadow
Broods dark the fate of Coll of Barisdale.
Strong of feature, loyal of step,
Who, at the call of Royalist vanity,
Led the pride of Knoydart men,
To the cannon's mouth,
On cursed Drumossie Moor.

And Piper's Isle, a tiny emerald isle, I anchored in it's lee,
A burn spread gravel on the shore,
I rode across, cupped water sweet and cool,
And in the crowning sun of Ladhar Ben.
I watched a pressing hind give birth,
And saw a knowing fox, await his cleansing fill,
Long weeks, I swam and climbed, lived the wildlife way.

One evening, rays of slanted yellow crossed on my sea green isle,
Stunted birch and heather clump, shelter rock and privacy,
Artic tern were nesting beside the noisy gull,
Three eggs, a scrape with pebble fringe,
First peck of gaping beak,
Was breaking through the shell,
Born to Black-back's hungry eye.

Crimson rich the Sound of Sleat,
Cuillin hills were ink pen cut,
Silence came as fading ripples on a shore
Are the edge of sleep.

And in that stillness terns took wing,
A curving, dipping trail,
Slender wing on dying sky,
A delicate rosy flight.

My boat was turning, drifting to the tide,
And about the boulders strewn,
Where orange weed lifted gently with the flood,
Two black shapes were twisting,
Lifting stones, tossing shells,
Playing, as the young will do,
At the fall of night.

Lithe black imps, I listened till the otter's whistle faded into dark.
Heavy the burden of our knowing,
Lost the peace of innocence,
Wisdom of their kind.

'Darling, think we've left it rather late, wish we'd built the house on stilts,
Artic melt's arriving at the door, but at least we've got the four-by four,
Head for the Med., there's always the boat,
Sad the roses have to float'.

Mind sets will be hard to shift, the comfy life, food provided by the poor,
Does it matter? Climate control is on the way, cut the sun's input two percent,
A dash more cloud cover? Volcanoes did it once before,
And science has some novel tricks in store.

Sulphur's cheap, fire some to the stratosphere, spread iron filings on the sea,
Better still, get tiny disc's into orbit, reflect sunlight back to space,
With twenty feet swilling across the lawns,
Land for food may be getting scarce.

Don't be silly, latest plan's are on the board, we're making artificial soil,
Mixing moon dust or maybe Martian debris with ammonium and potassium,
We'll need it for our new moon base,
Soil in space is on the way.

Goodbye the days of certainty, the inertia thinking that we're here to stay,
When voyagers sailed past Hercules, and Viking explored New Maines' shore,
They faced the challenge fresh insights bring,
This will tax imagination's core.

Space is no silent place, asteroids blast to smithereens, eruptions blot the Venus face,
And beyond, where the galaxies grind, is the fabled Music of the Spheres,
Sirens who bewitched the ancient men,
Their call is on the sea again.

Meantime back on earth, our current base, who will control this climate experiment?
The mass are busy with their holidays, they wont mind, if all goes well,
If not, is it vital our knowledge base survives?
What are we but a form of consciousness?

The cosmos is our canvas, the playground of biology, spawned in bygone space,
The outcome of quantum possibility, in a series of infinities,
That thinks it takes a universal overview,
Swops uncertainty for a probability.

Waiting in the wings, the conscious computer packs more kick in less DNA,
Caviar isn't on it's menu, doesn't lie on beaches, get melted by the sun,
Our biology flirts with the atoms in a primeval sea,
A Silicon Brain may yet control this Universe.

"Stop this 'sci-fi' rot my dear, get real, solve the problems at the ranch,
I know our six cylinder, cross country jeep pumps out the gas,
That's what three litre jobs always do, when they pass you see",
"But darling, the Jones have one, why shouldn't we?"

Lucky, Ethanol production is all the go, eats up acres, well, so,
Eck's out oil, keeps the cost of air conditioning in our cash flow,
Boom time farmers, corn fields waving cheques, fuel instead of bread,
Food and mouths are out of step, lifestyles deify the drought aid dead.

No sanitation, water half a mile, who wouldn't swop a camel for a motorcar?
Holidays from the hoe and paddy field, producing grub is such a chore,
Six billion plus at a recent count, scramble for the Yankee Dream,
Unless we turn sunshine into nourishment more efficiently,
Down sizing of our species is roaring up the motorway.

Have we tipped the climate scales? Running this planet off the rails?
Another three degrees, maybe more. As we tinker with controls,
Attempt to keep our lifestyles on the up,
Can we halt the melting poles?

Oscillations on a long term scale are no new planetary fad,
The sun plays tricks, friend or enemy, at six thousand degrees,
To think he's stable is this civilisation's grand delusion,
 And there's no plan yet to tame it's fusion.

Passing round a sand bucket won't put out the flames,
Too many heads are sticking in, till water's at the door,
Or they learn the stare of a cupboard bare.
Silicon Brain? It's intelligence now,
Instead of human greed.

The mainsheet's taut, wave tops crisp and clean,
The tiller has so little weight,
A length of cord will hold her straight,
Two-seventy degrees, the needle swings,
And through your head the music sings,
The hymn of life is on each crest,
Dawn is on your shoulder.
Soon the sun will warm your back,
Tinge the spray that feeds the air,
On the blood of day.

Clouds uncoil wild twisting shapes,
Mirror of the elemental
Cycle of events that drive us,
As the north wind fills my sail,
Unknowing of the tiller's hand,
Held as we, in the illusion of free will.

Sail on my bonnie boat,
Sail the fair wind's compass track,
Cross the Minch with me.
Blue isles lie below the sun of birth,
Mesmeric as the foetal motion,
Of the flowing sea.

The Long Island stretches land to sea,
And on the beaches of simplicity,
A body washed, symbol of war's folly,
A sailor's grave, name unknown,
Save to skylark song,
And the constant tide.

Long Island of the migrant soul,
Horizons of a dying sun,
Ever in the mind.

In mearured time our planet dies,
Held in the arms of a bay,
Who's mingled flesh still marks the void,
Where emotions hide in spirits free,
Beside a turquoise sea.

A sea who's simple waves uncurl,
To spread, and curl again,
As the photons of entanglement
Are the green swell of eternity.

And cosmos turn 'til night is day,
Fresh seas will surge, and flow, and urge,
And entwining life shall dream once more,
On the shores of an endless tide.